We Worship Here

CHRISTIAN CHURCH

Angela Wood ◦ Emma Trithart

Franklin Watts

First published in Great Britain in
2019 by The Watts Publishing Group

Credits
Series Editor: Sarah Peutrill
Series Designer: Anthony Hannant,
Little Red Ant

Text consultants:
Religious Education Consultant:
Margaret Barratt M.A.,
Religious Education Lecturer
Christianity Consultant: Alison
Seaman, Deputy Director, National
Society Religious Education
CentreReading Consultant: Prue
Goodwin, Reading and Language
Information Centre, Reading

ISBN 978 1 4451 6134 1

Printed in Dubai

Franklin Watts
An imprint of
Hachette Children's Group
Part of The Watts Publishing Group
Carmelite House
50 Victoria Embankment
London EC4Y 0DZ

An Hachette UK Company

www.hachette.co.uk
www.franklinwatts.co.uk

MIX
Paper from
responsible sources
FSC
www.fsc.org
FSC® C104740

CONTENTS

Words in **bold** are in the glossary on page 28.

CHURCHES AROUND THE WORLD

A **church** is a place where Christians go to worship **God**. There are many different kinds of Christian worship. There are churches all around the world.

This is an old church.

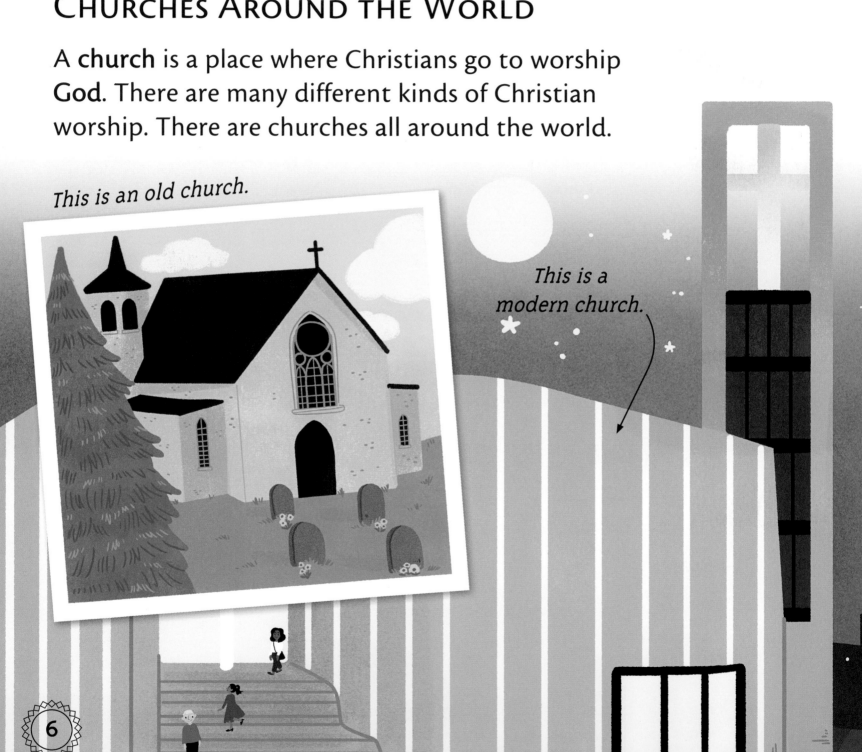

This is a modern church.

CHRISTIAN BELIEF

Christians believe in one God who created the world. He loved people so much that he sent his son, Jesus, to live among them.

This is Jesus with his mother, Mary.

Jesus

Jesus lived on Earth and helped people to understand about God. He taught people how to live together lovingly. Many of them did not understand who he was or the things he did. Because of this he was killed on a **cross**. Some churches have a statue of Jesus on a cross. This is called a **crucifix**.

When Christians see a crucifix they remember that Jesus loved them enough to die for them.

Most churches have a plain cross. Christians believe that three days after Jesus was buried he was alive again and with his followers. The cross tells Christians that Jesus did not die forever and that he is with them always.

There are often candles in churches. They remind Christians that Jesus was like a light to guide them.

Inside a Church

Churches can be plain or they can have a lot of pictures and objects with different meanings in them.

Often a priest, minister or preacher leads the worship at the front of the church.

THE ALTAR

Most churches have an **altar** or a communion table (see pages 20–21) in a place where everyone can see it. The altar may be attached to the wall or free-standing.

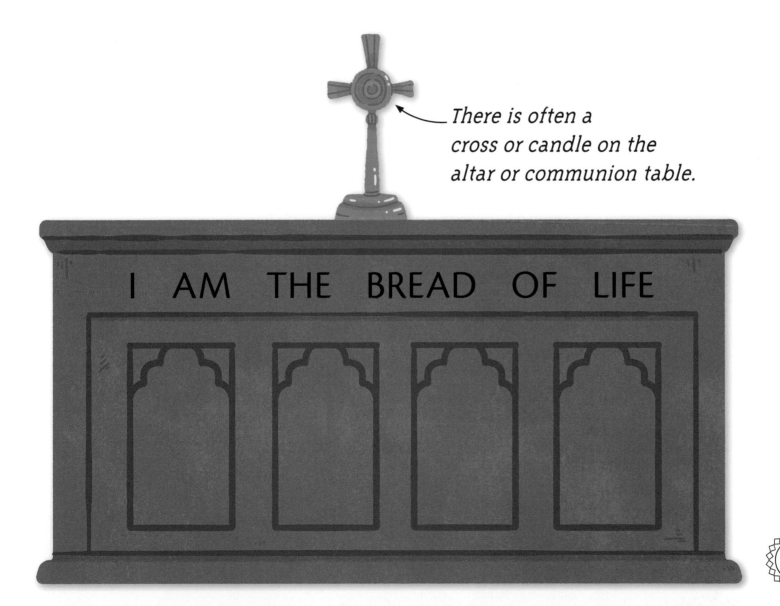

There is often a cross or candle on the altar or communion table.

I AM THE BREAD OF LIFE

THE BIBLE

There are always **Bibles** in a church. The Bible is the most important Christian book. It tells Christians about how God guided people before Jesus was born. It also describes Jesus, his teachings and the beginning of the Church. Many Christians have their own Bibles.

*This Orthodox minister, or deacon, is reading the Bible to the **congregation**.*

The Bible is often read from a stand called a lectern. This priest is kissing the Bible to show his respect for God's words.

13

THE SERMON

The preacher usually explains what the Bible means to Christians today. The talk is called a sermon.

The sermon helps Christians to think about what they believe.

The Windows

Some churches have beautiful windows with pictures made out of stained glass. They often tell stories from the Bible or show **saints**. (Saints are people who show their love for Jesus in special ways.)

BEING PART OF THE CHURCH

People often start life as a Christian by being **baptised**. This means they are **blessed** with **holy** water. In a church the water is often held in a **font**.

This Catholic woman blesses herself with holy water as she comes into a church.

Christians are baptised as babies or when they are grown up. This baby is being baptised at a font.

Christians feel that God is always with them. They call this the Holy Spirit. The Holy Spirit shows them how to love and help others. In some churches the Holy Spirit is shown as a dove or pictures of flames.

The dove stands for the Holy Spirit coming into the world. The circle is the world.

One way that Christians help others is by giving money to those in need. Often this is collected in the church.

A Church Service

The special day for most Christians is Sunday. Many churches have **services** on Sundays. This is when Christians gather together to share their love for God. In some churches there are lots of people and music plays an important part in the service. In others it is very quiet and still.

These children are sitting together in the church as they pray to God.

As part of a service, people say **prayers**. Prayers are a way that Christians speak and listen to God. Usually someone reads from the Bible. Everyone joins together to sing **hymns** that praise God. In some churches a **choir** leads the hymn singing.

Holy Communion

Some churches have a service called **Holy Communion**. The people eat a piece of bread and drink some wine or grape juice to remember the Last Supper (see page 11).

The minister blesses the bread and wine.
Then the people eat and drink them. They
think about how Jesus loves them.

In some churches, for example a Roman Catholic church, Holy Communion is called **Mass**. The priest uses wine and a wafer of special bread. Each wafer is called a **host**.

Tabernacle

The host is kept in a special place called the Tabernacle, behind the altar.

Children helping at the altar wear robes called vestments.

PRAYING ALONE

Sometimes Christians pray quietly to God on their own. This is a chance for them to think about what God means to them.

This man is praying in front of a special picture called an **icon**.

This woman is lighting a candle and saying a prayer while she kneels in front of a statue of Jesus.

Children in a Church

In many churches children help in different ways. On Sundays children can go to classes where they learn about being Christians and hear stories from the Bible.

These children are making a model as part of learning about a story from the Bible.

Children from a nearby school are in this church choir.

Often children read from the Bible during a service.

Glossary

altar a special table in a church on which Holy Communion or Mass is celebrated

baptised becoming a member of the Christian church by being blessed with holy water

Bible the special book for Christians

blessed when God has shown someone or something a special feeling or sign of his love

choir a group of singers in a church

church the place where Christians go to worship God and learn about the Christian faith

congregation the people at a church service

cross one of the signs of the Christian church because Jesus died on one

crucifix a cross that shows Jesus on it to remind Christians of his love for them

font a bowl to hold the holy water for a baptism

God known by Christians as the Father, Son and Holy Spirit

holy people who live their lives close to God, or special Christian places and times

Holy Communion a service that helps Christians feel close to God. In some Christian churches it is called Mass

host a round, thin piece of special bread

hymns songs sung to God

icon special religious images found in some churches

Mass a special service that helps Christians feel close to God. In some churches it is called Holy Communion

prayers when people listen and talk to God

saints holy people who live their lives for God

service a meeting of Christians in church

INDEX